# ALGORITHMS

## A Problem-Solving Journey

Help the alien return to his home planet by solving everyday problems quickly!

KUM⚬N

# Introduction

You may be wondering to yourself, "What is an algorithm?"

Though the word may be unfamiliar, you have seen algorithms in action already. There are a lot of things around you which are run by computers, such as smartphones, tablets, air conditioners, and refrigerators. In addition, many new inventions also use computers, like self-driving cars, drones, and artificial intelligence (AI).

Algorithms are a special way of thinking which can be used to write programs that make all of those computers run well. Depending on which algorithm you use, the time it takes the computer to complete a task can vary dramatically.

Use this book in two ways while you learn the basics of algorithms:

## 1 Enjoy solving the questions

We cut out the difficult parts, so even complete beginners can easily read this book. There may be parts you don't understand when you read the explanations, but you can skim through them. Firstly, you should enjoy solving the problems.

## 2 Learn for your future

Knowing various algorithms is useful when writing programs which make computers run well. In order to choose a suitable algorithm for a program, it is important to consider and understand each step of an algorithm. This book contains many questions which require careful reading and consideration.

This book is very useful for your future. Let's enjoy algorithms together!

**Project Lecturer of Osaka Electro-Communication University**
**Maiko Shimabuku**

# Contents

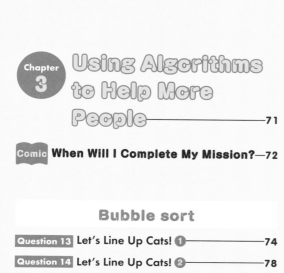

**Disclaimer**

This book was based on information available before February 2024 which may differ from the latest technology.

This book occasionally prioritizes ease of understanding, in consideration of education, over exactness.

We cannot answer any inquiries about technology beyond the scope of this book.

7

Yes! Using algorithms is an efficient way to solve problems!

What are they? I don't really know what they are. Please teach me!

Of course! We'll start with the basics.

First, let's go to where you crashed your spacecraft!

Wait for meeeee!!

# How to Use This Book

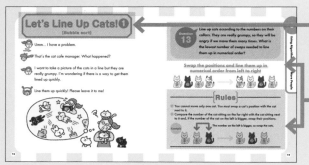

## ①Algorithm name

Remember the names and types of algorithms which are used in the questions.

## ②Question

Read the question and rules carefully, then solve the problem.

## ③Answer

Don't just check the answers, Read the explanations as well.

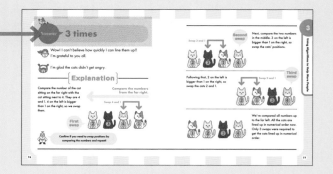

## ④Understanding more about algorithms

At the end of each chapter, we'll introduce some algorithm fundamentals as well as practical uses of the algorithms you learned in that chapter.

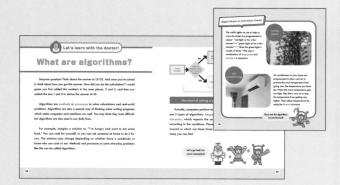

# Chapter 1

# Think in Order

It is important to have the right flow in your brain when learning about algorithms.
Let's help the aliens repair their spacecraft while learning the basic algorithms: Sequential, Iteration, and Branch.

# Let's Move Heavy Items ①
## [Sequential]

**Alien**: Wow! My spacecraft is stuck in some big rocks! I can't move it! I need to move the rocks.

**Chloe**: You landed quite dramatically.

**Doctor**: You will not be able to move these big rocks on your own. Let's ask QUICK to help move the rocks without breaking them.

## Question 1

We told QUICK to follow the instructions in the note. If QUICK moves as instructed, where will the spacecraft and the rocks end up? Choose from options (1) to (4).

**Note**

Pick up the top rock in the middle.
⬇
Put it on the right.
⬇
Pick up the top rock in the middle.
⬇
Put it on the right.

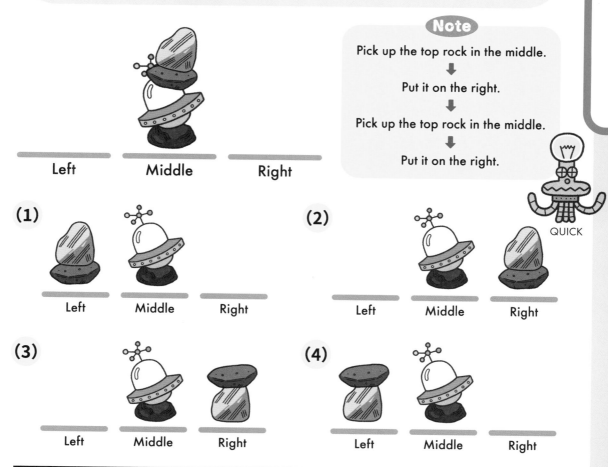

Left　　　Middle　　　Right

**(1)**

Left　　　Middle　　　Right

**(2)**

Left　　　Middle　　　Right

**(3)**

Left　　　Middle　　　Right

**(4)**

Left　　　Middle　　　Right

QUICK

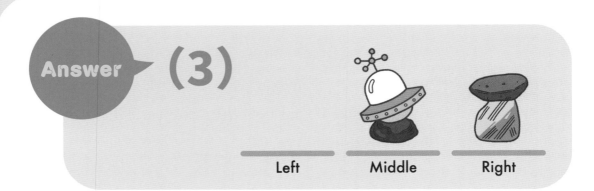

Left     Middle     Right

 Ahh, the rocks are moved one by one as the note instructed! Robots are so powerful.

 You have no time to be impressed!

## { Explanation }

**Note**

(1) Pick up the top rock in the middle.
    ⬇
(2)      Put it on the right.
    ⬇
(3) Pick up the top rock in the middle.
    ⬇
(4)      Put it on the right.

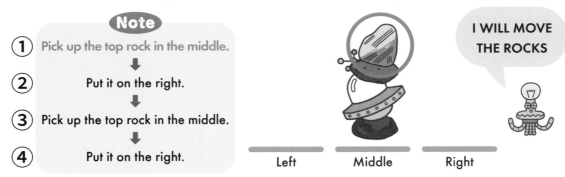

**I WILL MOVE THE ROCKS**

Left     Middle     Right

Let's move QUICK as the note instructs. According to instruction ①, QUICK picks up the top rock in the middle.

① Pick up the top rock in the middle.
↓
② Put it on the right.
↓
③ Pick up the top rock in the middle.
↓
④ Put it on the right.

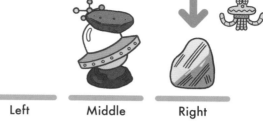

Left    Middle    Right

According to instruction ②, QUICK puts the rock on the right.

········································································

① Pick up the top rock in the middle.
↓
② Put it on the right.
↓
③ Pick up the top rock in the middle.
↓
④ Put it on the right.

Left    Middle    Right

According to instruction ③, QUICK picks up the top rock in the middle.

········································································

① Pick up the top rock in the middle.
↓
② Put it on the right.
↓
③ Pick up the top rock in the middle.
↓
④ Put it on the right.

Left    Middle    Right

According to instruction ④, QUICK puts the rock on the right to finish.

# Let's Move Heavy Items ② (Sequential)

 We've moved the rocks that are on top of the spacecraft.
But there are still rocks under it, so it's wobbly and unstable.

 There are so many rocks around here.
I wish we could put the spacecraft somewhere more stable.

 OK! Let's ask QUICK to move things again.

**Question 2**

We told QUICK to follow the instructions in the note. If QUICK moves as instructed, where will the spacecraft and the rocks end up? Choose from options (1) to (4).

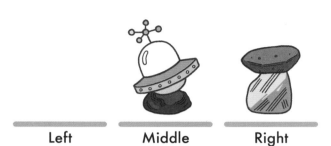

Left    Middle    Right

LOADING...
UH-HUH

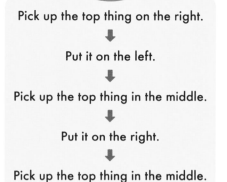

**Note**

Pick up the top thing on the right.

⬇

Put it on the left.

⬇

Pick up the top thing in the middle.

⬇

Put it on the right.

⬇

Pick up the top thing in the middle.

⬇

Put it on the left.

⬇

Pick up the top thing on the right.

⬇

Put it on the middle.

**(1)**

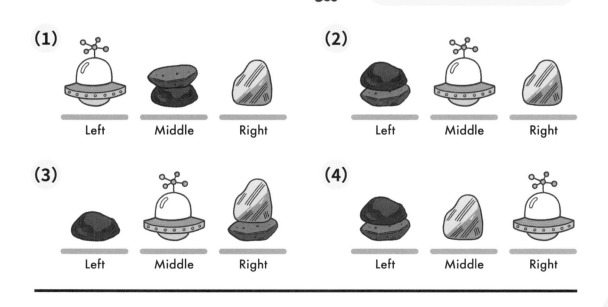

Left    Middle    Right

**(2)**

Left    Middle    Right

**(3)**

Left    Middle    Right

**(4)**

Left    Middle    Right

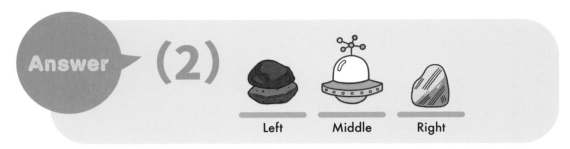

**Answer** — **(2)**

Left    Middle    Right

 There were more instructions than last time but if you work through them in order, it's not so difficult!

## { Explanation }

**Note**

① { Pick up the top thing on the right. ⬇ Put it on the left. }
⬇
② { Pick up the top thing in the middle. ⬇ Put it on the right. }
⬇
③ { Pick up the top thing in the middle. ⬇ Put it on the left. }
⬇
④ { Pick up the top thing on the right. ⬇ Put it on the middle. }

It's easier to understand if you think of the movements of picking up and putting down again as one set.

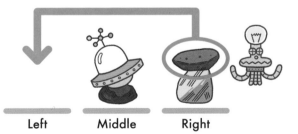

Left    Middle    Right

Let's move QUICK as the note instructs. According to instruction ①, QUICK picks up the top rock on the right and puts it down on the left.

② Pick up the top thing in the middle.
⬇
Put it on the right.

According to the instruction ②, QUICK picks up the spacecraft in the middle and puts it on top of the rock on the right.

③ Pick up the top thing in the middle.
⬇
Put it on the left.

According to instruction ③, QUICK picks up the top rock in the middle and puts it on top of the rock on the left.

④ Pick up the top thing on the right.
⬇
Put it on the middle.

According to instruction ④, QUICK picks up the spacecraft on the right and puts it on the middle to finish.

Hooray, I'm so relieved! The spacecraft should work now!
Huh? Even when I turn the engine on, it doesn't work! Why?

 Maybe it's run out of fuel?

 Well, it seems like some batteries are missing.
We need to add some new batteries to the spacecraft!

 The spacecraft is powered by batteries?!

**Question 3**

Add some batteries to the spacecraft. The spacecraft will not work if you don't have the batteries in the correct order. Which batteries should be in A and B? Choose from options (1) to (3).

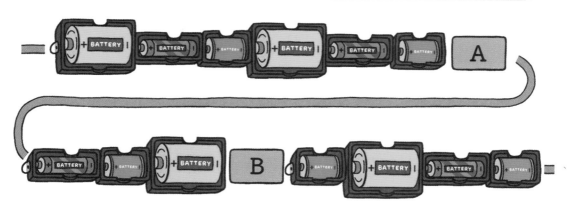

What order are the batteries in?

**(1)** Thick battery

**(2)** Small battery

**(3)** Thin battery

**Answer** → **A : (1) Thick battery**
**B : (3) Thin battery**

 I see how important it is to put them in the correct order!

─────── { **Explanation** } ───────

What order are the batteries in?

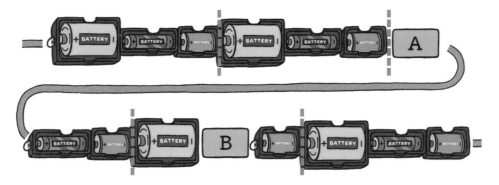

If you look carefully at the order, you can see that the batteries are in a repeating pattern of thick battery, thin battery, small battery.

**Battery order** → [battery] → [battery] → [battery]

Put batteries in the spaces marked A and B by following the order. There is a small battery before A, so the order will repeat and (1) the thick battery should go in.

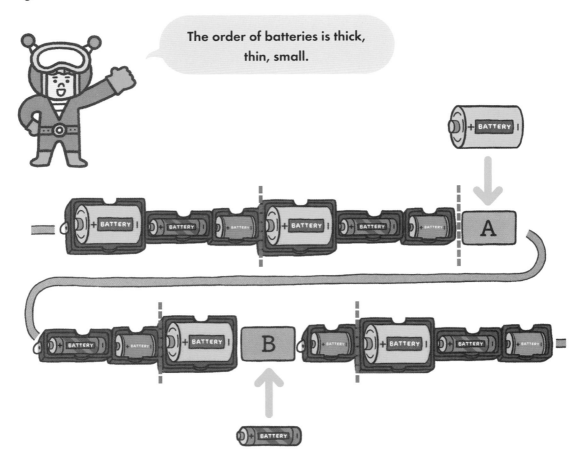

The order of batteries is thick, thin, small.

There is a thick battery before B, so (3) the thin battery should go in to maintain the order.

Look! There are also a lot of batteries lined up here! But some batteries are missing.

 I didn't know my spacecraft was powered by this many batteries! Amazing.

 Well, we need to put more batteries into the spacecraft again.

**Question 4**

**Add some batteries to the spacecraft. The spacecraft will not work if you don't have the batteries in the correct order. Which batteries should be in A, B and C? Choose from options (1) to (3).**

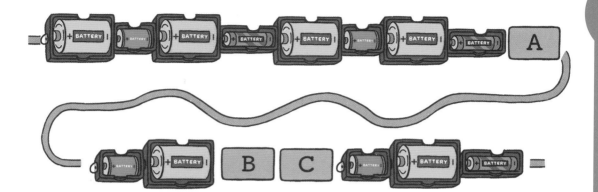

Don't overthink things.
Just look carefully at the order!

Uhhh... The order of the batteries is...

**(1) Small battery**

**(2) Thin battery**

**(3) Thick battery**

A : (3) Thick battery

B : (2) Thin battery

C : (3) Thick battery

 There are more batteries, so it's more complicated!

## { Explanation }

What order are the batteries in?

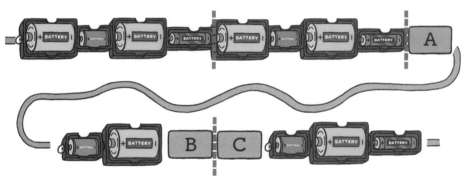

If you look carefully at the order, you can see that the batteries are in a repeating pattern of thick battery, small battery, thick battery, thin battery.

**Battery order**

Put batteries in spaces A, B, and C by following the order. There is a thin battery in front of A so the order will repeat and (3) the thick battery should go in.

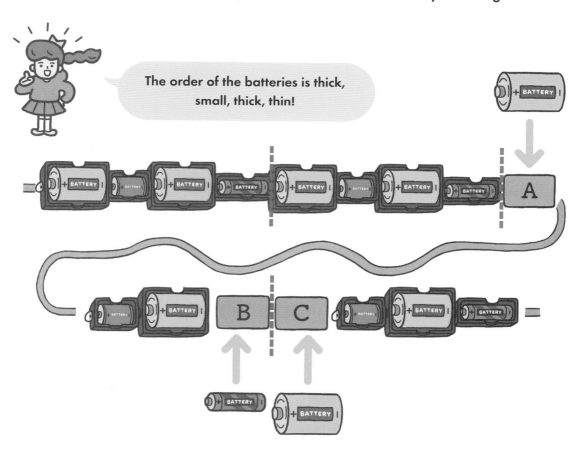

The order of the batteries is thick, small, thick, thin!

There is a small battery and a thick battery before B, so (2) the thin battery should go in to maintain the order. The order will repeat at C, so (3) the thick battery should go in.

# Let's Repair The Spacecraft ③
## [Branch]

 We added batteries, but the spacecraft still doesn't work.

 OMG. The spacecraft is broken!

 Well, there's an instruction manual with the spacecraft!
We can follow the instructions to use the spare parts and
repair the spacecraft!

**Question 5**

Choose the required parts to repair the broken spacecraft. If you choose parts by following the instruction manual, what combination should it be? Choose from options (1) to (3).

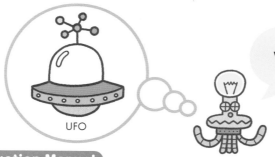

UFO

WE REPAIR QUICK!

**Box of bolts**

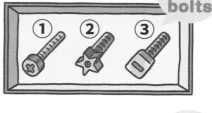

**Instruction Manual**

- If the shape of the spacecraft viewed from above is round, use a rectangular-headed bolt.
- If the shape of the spacecraft viewed from above is rectangular, use a round-headed bolt.
- If the shape of the spacecraft viewed from above is a star, use a star-headed bolt.

**Box of rods**

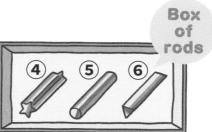

**Instruction Manual**

- If the antenna has one light bulb, use a circular rod.
- If the antenna has three light bulbs, use a triangular rod.
- If the antenna has five light bulbs, use a star-shaped rod.

(1) ①, ⑤          (2) ③, ④          (3) ③, ⑥

31

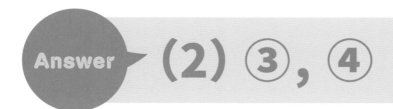

**Answer** ▸ **(2) ③, ④**

 So you choose each part according to each shape.
But can we actually repair the spacecraft?

 Don't worry. Leave it to me!

## ⎰ Explanation ⎱

Choose the required parts according to the conditions in the instruction manual.
Viewed from above, the spacecraft looks round, so you should choose a
rectangular headed bolt from the box of bolts.

View from above

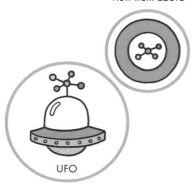

UFO

**Instruction Manual**

✓ If the shape of the spacecraft viewed from above is
round, use a rectangular-headed bolt.

✗ If the shape of the spacecraft viewed from above is
rectangular, use a round-headed bolt.

✗ If the shape of the spacecraft viewed from above is a
star, use a star-headed bolt.

The antenna has five light bulbs, so you should choose a star-shaped rod from the box of rods.

Look for the appropriate parts in each box. "The rectangular headed bolt" is ③, and "star-shaped rod " is ④, so the answer is (1).

Box of bolts

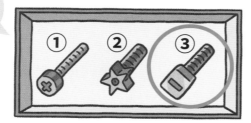

Box of rods

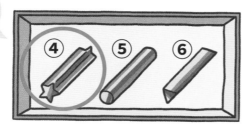

EASY EASY!

# Let's Repair The Spacecraft ④
## [Branch]

 I didn't know spaceships were made of so many different parts.

 My father made it for me. Amazing, isn't it?

 Stop chatting and get to work!
Could you bring some more parts?

**Question 6**

**Choose the parts needed to repair the broken spacecraft. If you choose parts by following the instruction manual, what combination should it be? Choose from options (1) to (3).**

**YOU NEED TO REMEMBER THE CHARACTERISTICS OF THE SPACECRAFT!**

UFO

**Instruction Manual**

- If the antenna has two light bulbs, use an L-shaped bracket.
- If the antenna has three light bulbs, use a straight bracket.
- If the antenna has five light bulbs, use a cross-shaped bracket.

Box of brackets

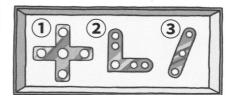

**Instruction Manual**

- If the shape of the spacecraft viewed from above is a star, use a thick spring.
- If the shape of the spacecraft viewed from above is round, use a curved spring.
- If the shape of the spacecraft viewed from above is a rectangle, use a long, thin spring.

Box of springs

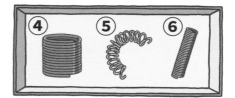

**Instruction Manual**

- If the antenna light bulbs are star-shaped, use a gear with no holes.
- If the antenna light bulbs are round, use a gear with fine teeth.
- If there are no light bulbs on the antenna, use a gear with 7 holes in it.

Box of gears

(1) ②, ⑤, ⑧　　(2) ①, ⑥, ⑧　　(3) ①, ⑤, ⑨

**Answer** **(3)** ① , ⑤ , ⑨

 Doctor! I brought the parts!

 Great, we'll be able to repair the spacecraft!

## { Explanation }

Choose the required parts according to the conditions in the instruction manual.
The antenna has five light bulbs, so choose the cross-shaped bracket.

**Instruction Manual**

✕ If the antenna has two light bulbs, use an L-shaped bracket.
✕ If the antenna has three light bulbs, use a straight bracket.
✓ If the antenna has five light bulbs, use a cross-shaped bracket.

UFO

Box
of
brackets

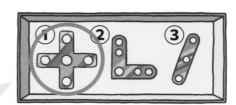

Next, choose the correct spring. The shape of the spacecraft viewed from above is round, so choose the curved spring.

**Instruction Manual**

✕ If the shape of the spacecraft viewed from above is a star, use a thick spring.

✓ If the shape of the spacecraft viewed from above is round, use a curved spring.

✕ If the shape of the spacecraft viewed from above is a rectangle, use a long, thin spring.

Box of springs

We need to make our choices by following the conditions.

Finally, choose a gear. The antenna light bulbs are rounded so choose the gear with fine teeth.

**Instruction Manual**

✕ If the antenna light bulbs are star-shaped, use a gear with no holes.

✓ If the antenna light bulbs are round, use a gear with fine teeth.

✕ If there are no light bulbs on the antenna, use a gear with 7 holes in it.

Box of gears

Bracket ①, spring ⑤ and gear ⑨ so the answer is (1).

# What are algorithms?

Surprise question! Think about the answer to 12+33. And once you've solved it, think about how you got the answer. How did you do the calculation? I would guess you first added the numbers in the ones places, 2 and 3, and then you added the tens 1 and 3 to derive the answer of 45.

Algorithms are methods or processes to solve calculations and real-world problems. Algorithms are also a special way of thinking when writing programs which make computers and machines run well. You may think they look difficult, but algorithms are also used in our daily lives.

For example, imagine a solution to, "I'm hungry and want to eat some food." You can cook for yourself, or you can ask someone at home to do it for you. The solution may change depending on whether there is somebody at home who can cook or not. Methods and processes to solve everyday problems like this can be called algorithms.

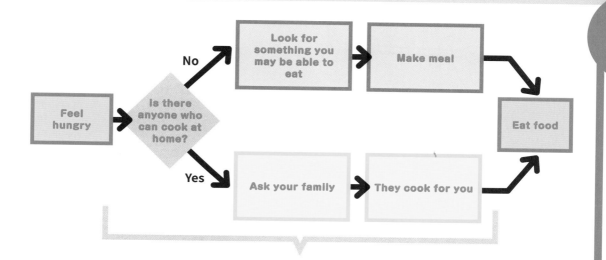

**Flowchart of solving a problem. (Think about the process)**

Actually, computers perform tasks step by step just as humans do. Computers use 3 types of algorithms: Sequential, which does things in a certain order, Iteration, which repeats the same task and Branch, which changes path according to the conditions. There are a lot of machines and home appliances around us which use these three structures. Have a look around to see how many you can find.

Let's go look for some examples!

## Algorithms in everyday items

The traffic lights we use to help us cross the street are programmed to repeat "red light on for a few minutes"→ "green light on for a few minutes" → "flash the green light a couple of times." This uses a combination of Sequential and Iteration in sequence.

**Traffic lights**

**Air conditioning**

Air conditioners in your home are programmed to blow cool air to prevent the room temperature from going over the temperature you have set. When the room temperature gets too high, they blow cool air to stop the temperature from getting any higher. They adjust temperatures by using the Branch structure.

These are the algorithms we just learned!

# Chapter 2

# Using Algorithms to Help People

We've got three new types of algorithms to learn:
Binary search algorithm, Breadth-first search,
and Facility location problems.
Make sure you read the questions and rules carefully.

# Let's Become a Number Guessing Master (1)
### [Binary search algorithm]

 Amelia, what are you worrying about?

 A popular game in class where you have to guess birthdays! I'm really unlucky and I always lose. How can I guess the right date more quickly?

Amelia

 That game does not depend on luck. You can reduce the range of possible answers little by little. All right, let's try using algorithms.

 It's great that you can also use algorithms here!

**Question 7**

Let's play a game of guessing birth months. The alien and Amelia have different methods for finding the answer. Who can get to the right answer more quickly?

**The alien's method**

I'll guess the middle number of 1–12, which is 6. If the answer is higher, I'm going to guess the middle number of 7–12. I'll repeat this until I find the answer.

**Answerer**

My birth month is November (11).

**Amelia's method**

I'll start from 1 and guess numbers one-by-one.

**(1) Amelia**     **(2) The alien**     **(3) Same**

## {Rules}

- If you have an even number of possible answers left, take the lower middle number as your guess.
- The answerer can only answer "correct," "higher," or "lower" for the numbers they were asked.

**Example**    Is it 3?     It's higher than 3.

Wow! I didn't know this method!

## { Explanation }

Think about how many times you need to guess to reach the right answer using the alien's method. This is a method to halve the range of possible answers with each guess.

**1st guess** Guess the middle number between 1–12.

Alien

Is it 6?    It's higher than 6.

1 2 3 4 5 6 7 8 9 10 11 12 → 1 2 3 4 5 6 7 8 9 10 11 12

**2nd guess** The right answer is higher than 6, so guess the middle number between 7–12.

Is it 9?    It's higher than 9.

1 2 3 4 5 6 7 8 9 10 11 12 → 1 2 3 4 5 6 7 8 9 10 11 12

**3rd guess** The right answer is higher than 9, so guess the middle number between 10–12.

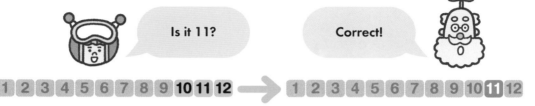

The alien found the right answer in 3 guesses.

........................................................................................

Next, let's use Amelia's method. Start from 1 and guess numbers one-by-one.

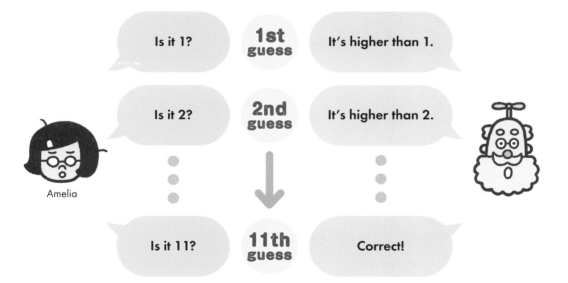

Amelia found the right answer in 11 guesses. The alien (2) found the right answer quicker, by making only 3 guesses.

# Let's Become a Number Guessing Master ②

## [Binary search algorithm]

 I can't believe you can get to the right answer so quickly! Can I try again?

 Of course! How do you feel, you two? You can solve problems quickly if you use algorithms.

 You're right, doctor! We can find answers efficiently if we use algorithms. I'm going to master them!

 I want to learn them too!!

**Question 8**

Let's play a game of guessing someone's date of birth. Amelia and Chloe have different methods for getting the answer. Who can get to the right answer more quickly?

**Answerer**

My date of birth is the 9th.

I'll guess the middle number of 1–30, which is 15. If the answer is higher, I'm going to guess the middle number of 16–30. I'll repeat this until I find the answer.

**Amelia's method**

I'm going to start from 1 and guess numbers one-by-one.

**Chloe's method**

**(1) Amelia   (2) Chloe   (3) Same**

## {Rules}

- If you have an even number of possible answers left, take the lower middle number as your guess.
- The answerer can only answer "correct," "higher," or "lower" for the numbers they were asked.

**Example**

Is it 5?

It's higher than 5.

## Answer ▸ (1) Amelia

 I may be able to become top in my class! Thank you very much for teaching me!

## { Explanation }

Think about how many times you need to guess to reach the right answer using Amelia's method. This is a method to halve the range of possible answers with each guess.

**1st guess** Guess the middle number between 1–30.

Amelia

Is it 15?

```
 1  2  3  4  5  6  7  8  9 10
11 12 13 14 15 16 17 18 19 20
21 22 23 24 25 26 27 28 29 30
```

It's smaller than 15.

· · · · · · · · · · · · · · · · · · · · · · · · · · · · · · · · · · · · · · · · · · · · · · · · · · · · · · · · · · · ·

**2nd guess** The right answer is smaller than 15, so guess the middle number between 1–14.

Is it 7?

```
 1  2  3  4  5  6  7  8  9 10
11 12 13 14 15 16 17 18 19 20
21 22 23 24 25 26 27 28 29 30
```

It's higher than 7.

**3rd guess** The right answer is bigger than 7, so guess the middle number between 8–14.

Is it 11?

| 1 | 2 | 3 | 4 | 5 | 6 | 7 | **8** | **9** | **10** |
| **11** | **12** | **13** | **14** | 15 | 16 | 17 | 18 | 19 | 20 |
| 21 | 22 | 23 | 24 | 25 | 26 | 27 | 28 | 29 | 30 |

It's lower than 11.

| 1 | 2 | 3 | 4 | 5 | 6 | 7 | **8** | **9** | **10** |
| 11 | 12 | 13 | 14 | 15 | 16 | 17 | 18 | 19 | 20 |
| 21 | 22 | 23 | 24 | 25 | 26 | 27 | 28 | 29 | 30 |

**4th guess** The right answer is smaller than 11, so guess the middle number between 8–10.

Is it 9?

| 1 | 2 | 3 | 4 | 5 | 6 | 7 | **8** | **9** | **10** |
| 11 | 12 | 13 | 14 | 15 | 16 | 17 | 18 | 19 | 20 |
| 21 | 22 | 23 | 24 | 25 | 26 | 27 | 28 | 29 | 30 |

Correct!

| 1 | 2 | 3 | 4 | 5 | 6 | 7 | 8 | **9** | 10 |
| 11 | 12 | 13 | 14 | 15 | 16 | 17 | 18 | 19 | 20 |
| 21 | 22 | 23 | 24 | 25 | 26 | 27 | 28 | 29 | 30 |

Amelia found the right answer in 4 guesses.

Is it 1? **1st guess** It's higher than 1.

Chloe

Is it 9? **9th guess** Correct!

It took Chloe 9 guesses to find the right answer guessing numbers one-by-one. Amelia found the right answer with her 4th guess, so the answer is **(1) Amelia**.

# Let's Finish The Maze First ①
## (Breadth-first search)

Boy

Excuse me. Do you know the strategy for this game?
It's a maze game and I have a competition soon.

A game competition? Sounds fun!
Although I've never played an Earth game.

I really want the premium card you can get if you win...
What should I do?

Well well, let's use algorithms again!

Maze King

Question
9

What's the shortest route to get out of this maze from the start (S) to the goal (G)?

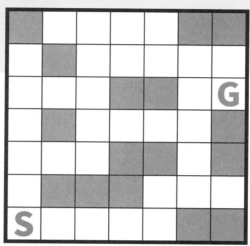

## {Rules}

● It takes 1 minute to move 1 square.
● You can only move 1 square vertically or horizontally from your current square. You cannot move diagonally. You cannot go into the gray squares.

Example

Write 0 on the start square and write 1 on the squares next to it. Write 2 on the squares next to the 1 squares. Repeat this pattern and you can find out how long it takes to get to the goal.

**10 minutes**

 I didn't know how useful this method was! I think I can do it!

——————— { **Explanation** } ———————

Once you've got 0 on the start square, write 1 in the squares next to it and 2 in the squares next to the 1s. Continue like this until you reach the goal.

Remember you cannot move diagonally, so be careful when writing the numbers.

| 5 | | | | | | |
|---|---|---|---|---|---|---|
| 4 | 5 | | | | | G |
| 3 | | 5 | | | | |
| 2 | 3 | 4 | | | | |
| 1 | | | | 5 | | |
| 0 | 1 | 2 | 3 | 4 | | |

Once all the squares are filled in, the squares next to the goal are 9 and 11.

| | 9 | 8 | 9 | 10 | | |
|---|---|---|---|---|---|---|
| 5 | | 7 | 8 | 9 | 10 | 11 |
| 4 | 5 | 6 | | | 9 | G |
| 3 | | 5 | 6 | 7 | 8 | |
| 2 | 3 | 4 | | | 7 | |
| 1 | | | | 5 | 6 | 7 |
| 0 | 1 | 2 | 3 | 4 | | |

As the lowest number next to the goal is 9, the goal square is 10.

The shortest time it takes to reach the goal of this maze is 10 minutes.

*Both of the below highlighted routes are correct.

| | 9 | 8 | 9 | 10 | | |
|---|---|---|---|---|---|---|
| 5 | | 7 | 8 | 9 | 10 | 11 |
| 4 | 5 | 6 | | | 9 | 10 |
| 3 | | 5 | 6 | 7 | 8 | |
| 2 | 3 | 4 | | | 7 | |
| 1 | | | | 5 | 6 | 7 |
| 0 | 1 | 2 | 3 | 4 | | |

| | 9 | 8 | 9 | 10 | | |
|---|---|---|---|---|---|---|
| 5 | | 7 | 8 | 9 | 10 | 11 |
| 4 | 5 | 6 | | | 9 | 10 |
| 3 | | 5 | 6 | 7 | 8 | |
| 2 | 3 | 4 | | | 7 | |
| 1 | | | | 5 | 6 | 7 |
| 0 | 1 | 2 | 3 | 4 | | |

# Let's Finish The Maze First ❷

## [Breadth-first search]

 You can find the shortest route using algorithms like this!

 Amazing! You are so knowledgeable. I was right to get advice from you.

 Earth games are so interesting! I'm into them.

 Looks fun. I'd like to try next time.

 Are you listening to me?

**Question 10**

**What's the shortest route to get out of the maze on the right from the start (S) to the goal (G)?**

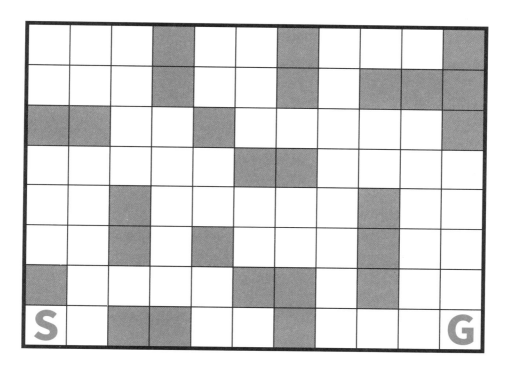

## {Rules}

- It takes 1 minute to move 1 square.
- You can only move 1 square vertically or horizontally from your current square. You cannot move diagonally. You cannot go into the gray squares.

All right! I put 0 on the start and fill in the numbers from there.

I really appreciate you teaching me this amazing method!
I may be able to win the competition.

 Go for it! I'm rooting for you!

───────── { **Explanation** } ─────────

Once you've got 0 on the start square, write 1 in the squares next to it and 2 in the squares next to the 1s. Continue like this until you reach the goal.

|   |   | 7 |   |   |   |   |   |   |   |   |
|---|---|---|---|---|---|---|---|---|---|---|
|   |   |   |   |   |   |   |   |   |   |   |
|   |   | 7 |   |   |   |   |   |   |   |   |
| 6 | 5 | 6 | 7 |   |   |   |   |   |   |   |
| 5 | 4 |   | 6 | 7 |   |   |   |   |   |   |
| 4 | 3 |   | 5 |   |   |   |   |   |   |   |
|   | 2 | 3 | 4 | 5 |   |   |   |   |   |   |
| 0 | 1 |   |   | 6 | 7 |   |   |   | G |   |

Once all the squares are filled in, the squares next to the goal are 15 and 17.

| 11 | 10 | 9 |   | 17 | 16 |   | 14 | 15 | 16 |   |
|----|----|----|----|----|----|----|----|----|----|----|
| 10 | 9 | 8 |   | 16 | 15 |   | 13 |   |   |   |
|   |   | 7 | 8 |   | 14 | 13 | 12 | 13 | 14 |   |
| 6 | 5 | 6 | 7 | 8 |   |   | 11 | 12 | 13 | 14 |
| 5 | 4 |   | 6 | 7 | 8 | 9 | 10 |   | 14 | 15 |
| 4 | 3 |   | 5 |   | 9 | 10 | 11 |   | 15 | 16 |
|   | 2 | 3 | 4 | 5 |   |   | 12 |   | 16 | 17 |
| 0 | 1 |   |   | 6 | 7 |   | 13 | 14 | 15 | G |

As the lowest number next to the goal is 15, the goal square is 16.
The shortest time it takes to reach the goal is 16 minutes.

| 11 | 10 | 9 |   | 17 | 16 |   | 14 | 15 | 16 |   |
|----|----|----|----|----|----|----|----|----|----|----|
| 10 | 9 | 8 |   | 16 | 15 |   | 13 |   |   |   |
|   |   | 7 | 8 |   | 14 | 13 | 12 | 13 | 14 |   |
| 6 | 5 | 6 | 7 | 8 |   |   | 11 | 12 | 13 | 14 |
| 5 | 4 |   | 6 | 7 | 8 | 9 | 10 |   | 14 | 15 |
| 4 | 3 |   | 5 |   | 9 | 10 | 11 |   | 15 | 16 |
|   | 2 | 3 | 4 | 5 |   |   | 12 |   | 16 | 17 |
| 0 | 1 |   |   | 6 | 7 |   | 13 | 14 | 15 | 16 |

* Any route you can follow to reach the goal in 16 minutes is fine.

# Let's Install Mailboxes ❶
## [Facility location problems]

**Man**

Excuse me. I have a problem!

How can I help you?

Wow! You're wearing interesting clothes. Well, I have something I want to ask. There is a plan to install new mailboxes around here, but where do you think we should place them? Is it fine just to place them randomly?

Wait a minute! You can't just do it randomly. How about trying algorithms?

**Question 11**

There is a plan to increase the number of mailboxes in town. But the mailboxes are expensive, so we can't install many of them. Which two places should we choose for the new mailboxes so that you can reach one from any station without passing through another station? Choose from options ① to ⑤.

## Plan of possible locations for mailboxes

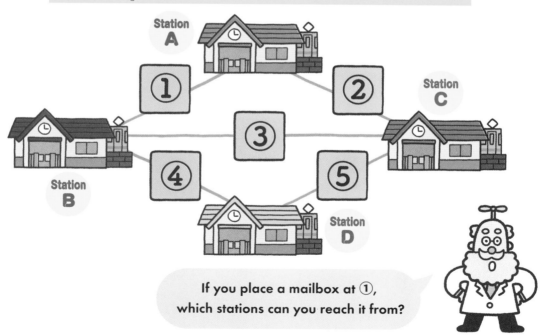

Station A

Station C

Station B

Station D

If you place a mailbox at ①, which stations can you reach it from?

Ahh!! Now I know the right places!

 Great! Don't say that random places are fine anymore!

## { Explanation }

Look for the places where mailboxes are required. Locations ①&② are next to station A. If we install a mailbox at ①, station A doesn't need another one at ②. Also, station B doesn't need a mailbox at ④ if there is the one at ①.

Either side is fine, so we'll install a mailbox at ①.

Next, install a mailbox between stations C and D. If placed at ⑤, it can be reached from both stations, so other mailboxes aren't required at ②, ③, or ④. Now we know if there are mailboxes at ①&⑤, they can be reached from all stations without passing through another station.

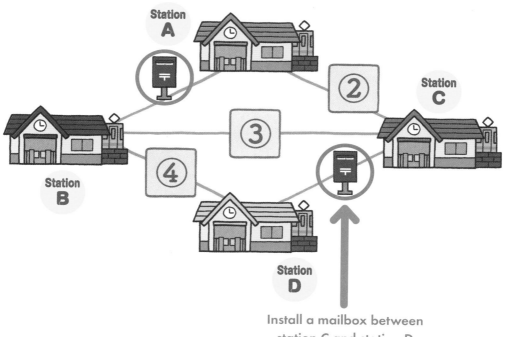

Install a mailbox between
station C and station D

Similarly, installing mailboxes at ②&④ is also correct.

# Let's Install Mailboxes ❷

## [Facility location problems]

 You guys are so clever! I respect your talent and I have another favor to ask. We need to install mailboxes in the next town too, but I don't know where to place them.

 Leave it to me! I'll solve your problem quickly!

 You're so helpful! I might get in trouble with my manager if I don't complete this task.

 Wow, the world of adults is tough...

**Question 12**

There is a plan to increase the number of mailboxes in the next town. Each station should be able to reach a mailbox without passing through another station. How many mailboxes should we install? Choose from options ① to ⑦.

# Plan of possible locations for mailboxes

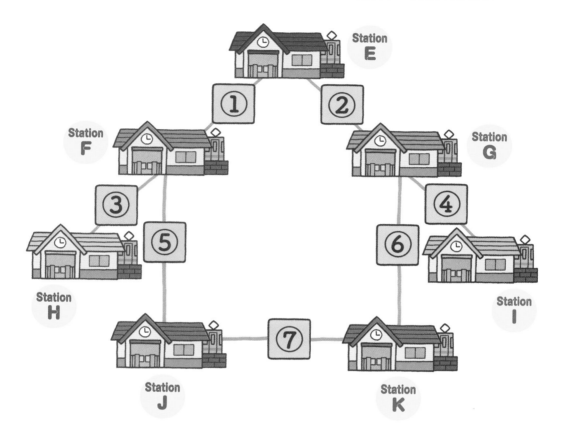

Which locations need mailboxes? We can't install a lot of them, so let's find the smallest number!

**Answer** **4** $\left(\begin{array}{l}①, ③, ④, ⑦ \text{ or} \\ ②, ③, ④, ⑦\end{array}\right)$

 You've really helped me out! I can report this to my manager! Thank you very much.

 Earth jobs are so tough. Good luck!

## Explanation

First, look for the places where mailboxes are definitely needed. Stations H and I have only one direct connection each, so we need to install mailboxes at ③&④.

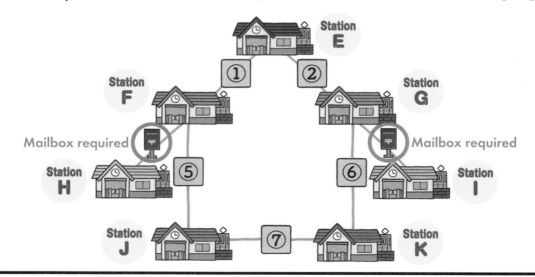

Next, install a mailbox between stations J and K at ⑦. So far, stations F, G, H, I, J, and K can all access a mailbox directly, so there is no need for ones at ⑤ or ⑥.

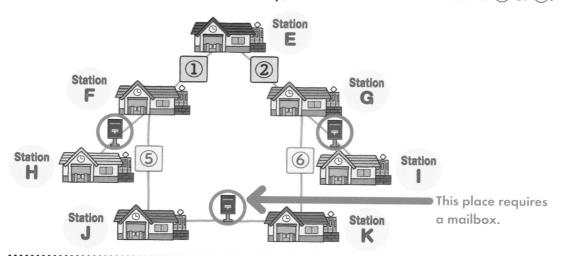

This place requires a mailbox.

Station E requires a mailbox at either ① or ②. 4 mailboxes are required in total.

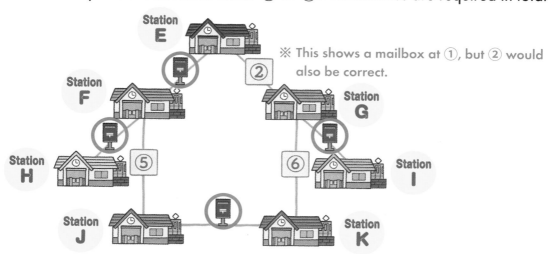

※ This shows a mailbox at ①, but ② would also be correct.

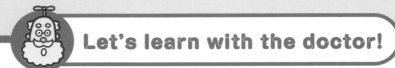

# Let's represent algorithms with diagrams

You can represent the steps of an algorithm in a figure called a flowchart. Let's make flowcharts to represent Sequential, Iteration, and Branch algorithms, as we learned in Chapter 1. For example, the steps for "Going out" and "Cleaning" are shown in the flowcharts below.

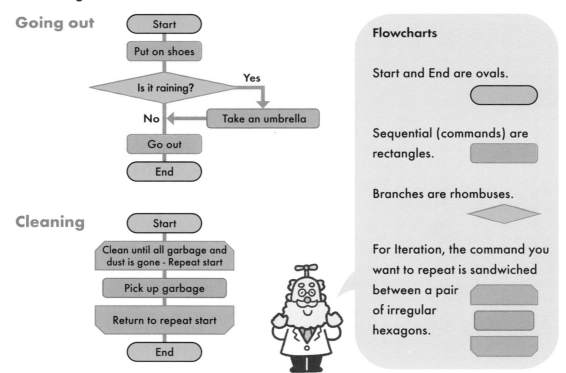

**Going out**

Start
Put on shoes
Is it raining? — Yes → Take an umbrella
No
Go out
End

**Cleaning**

Start
Clean until all garbage and dust is gone - Repeat start
Pick up garbage
Return to repeat start
End

**Flowcharts**

Start and End are ovals.

Sequential (commands) are rectangles.

Branches are rhombuses.

For Iteration, the command you want to repeat is sandwiched between a pair of irregular hexagons.

In Chapter 2, we studied an algorithm to find target information from a large amount of information (binary search algorithm) and an algorithm to place a thing in the best position (p. 60 Facility location problems).

In the binary search question (p. 44) we saw a method for finding an answer by starting at 1 and searching one-by-one. This is an algorithm called linear search. You can find information faster with linear search if the information you are looking for is close to the beginning. However, if the information is around the middle or latter half, binary search is faster. The purpose of both methods (finding the information quickly) is the same, but the time it takes to find the information can vary.

These algorithms can be illustrated by flowcharts. For example, a flowchart representing binary search, "Finding a card from cards in numerical order" is illustrated below.

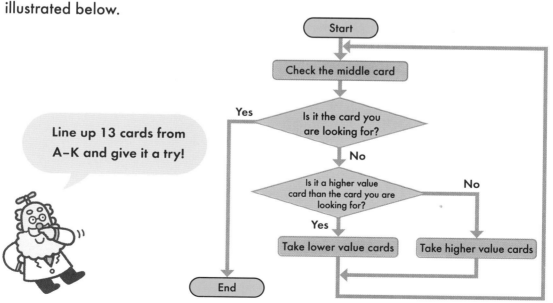

Search engines like Google search through a vast number of websites and show you sites relating to the keywords you entered.

Search algorithms such as binary search are used here. These algorithms are improved every day to be able to look for information more efficiently.

**Search engines**

# Search

**Location of base stations**

Smartphones connect to nearby base stations so you can make calls and use the internet. The placement of base stations is really important because they enable you to use your smartphone wherever you are.
Facility location problems are used to determine the best number and location of base stations.

I think I've seen them around town!

# Chapter 3

# Using Algorithms to Help More People

And now for three more algorithms:
Bubble sort, Selection sort,
Dijkstra's algorithm, and Caesar cipher!
It's not so difficult if you think step-by-step,
just like you have been doing this whole time.

Have you started understanding algorithms?

Yes! Little by little!

I thought I was just slow but I've realized that my methods and processes for finding solutions were wrong.

You're right. If you make a mistake, you can just look for the cause and start again from the place where you went wrong.

Life is like an algorithm...

Huh?? Did I say something weird?

Yes!

What?!?

LIFE...?

# Let's Line Up Cats! ①
## [Bubble sort]

Store manager

Umm... I have a problem.

That's the cat cafe manager. What happened?

I want to take a picture of the cats in a line but they are really grumpy. I'm wondering if there is a way to get them lined up quickly.

Line them up quickly? Please leave it to me!

## Question 13

Line up the cats according to the numbers on their collars. They are really grumpy, so they will be angry if we move them too many times. What is the lowest number of swaps needed to line them up in numerical order?

## Swap the positions and line them up in numerical order from left to right

    →

## {Rules}

- You cannot move only one cat. You must swap a cat's position with the cat next to it.
- Compare the number of the cat sitting on the far right with the cat sitting next to it and, if the number of the cat on the left is bigger, swap their positions.

Example

The number on the left is bigger, so swap the cats.

  →

**Answer** **3 times**

 Wow! I can't believe how quickly I can line them up!! I'm grateful to you all.

 I'm glad the cats didn't get angry.

--- { **Explanation** } ---

Compare the number of the cat sitting on the far right with the cat sitting next to it. They are 4 and 1. 4 on the left is bigger than 1 on the right, so we swap them.

**Compare the numbers from the far right.**

Swap 4 and 1

 **First swap**

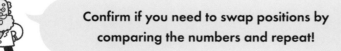 Confirm if you need to swap positions by comparing the numbers and repeat!

Swap 3 and 1

**Second swap**

Next, compare the two numbers in the middle. 3 on the left is bigger than 1 on the right, so swap the cats' positions.

Following that, 2 on the left is bigger than 1 on the right, so swap the cats 2 and 1.

Swap 2 and 1

**Third swap**

We've compared all numbers up to the far left. All the cats are lined up in numerical order now. Only 3 swaps were required to get the cats lined up in numerical order.

Thank you very much! Actually... I have another request.

 Don't tell me you have more cats to line up?

 That's right. Some of them are hiding in the back of the room. Can I get them lined up quickly like last time?

**Question 14**

**Line up cats according to the numbers on their collars. They are really grumpy so change their positions quickly to avoid making them angry. What is the lowest number of swaps needed to line them up in numerical order?**

 Swap the positions and line them up in numerical order from left to right.

# {Rules}

○ You cannot move only one cat. You must swap a cat's position with the cat next to it.

○ Compare the number of the cat sitting next to each other and, if the number of the cat on the left is bigger, swap their positions.

○ Once you've reached the far left, go back to the far right and compare the numbers again.

○ Repeat this process until all the cats are lined up in numerical order.

**First time**        **Compare numbers from the far right.**

**Second time**      **Go back to the far right and compare the numbers again.**

**Example**

It looks difficult because the number of cats has increased.

It's ok. Just compare the numbers next to each other as you did last time.

**Answer** ▶ **3 times**

 I can't believe the cats were so calm this whole time. I think I can take some good pictures now! Thanks!

---

## { Explanation }

Compare the number of the cat sitting on the far right with the cat sitting next to it. First, they are 5 and 4. 5 on the left is bigger, so swap the cats.

**Compare numbers from the far right.**

Swap 5 and 4

**First swap**

---

Next is 2 and 4. 4 on the right is bigger, so there is no need to swap them. Next is 1 and 2. 2 on the right is bigger, so there is no need to swap them.

Swap 3 and 1

**Second swap**

Next is 3 and 1. 3 on the left is bigger, so swap them. We've compared all the numbers to the far left, so we now know that 1 in this position is the smallest number in this series.

Compare the numbers from the far right again. Comparing 4 and 5, 5 on the right is bigger, so no swap is required. No need to swap 2 and 4 for the same reason.

**Go back to the far right and compare numbers**

Confirmed

**Third swap**

Swap 3 and 2

Next is 3 and 2. 3 on the left is bigger, so swap them. 1 has been confirmed on the far left so no comparison is required. Finally, all the cats are lined up in numerical order.

# Let's Rearrange Books ①
## [Selection sort]

Grandpa
Ouch... My back hurts!

Are you ok? I can help you!

That would be helpful. I want to rearrange the books on the top shelf but my back hurts... ouch!

I think we can do that! We'll help you!

82

Question

## Question 15

Rearrange the randomly ordered books so they are in ascending order. If you follow the rules, what is the lowest number of swaps needed to line up the books in numerical order?

## Swap books and line them up in ascending order from left to right.

---

# {Rules}

- Find the book with the smallest number and swap it with the book on the far left.
- Among the remaining books, find the book with the smallest number and again swap it with the book on the far left. Repeat until all the books are lined up in order.

**Example**  Find the book with the smallest number and swap it with the book on the far left

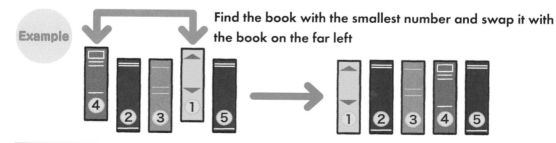

**Answer** 3 times

I was lucky that you were passing by when I had a problem.

## { Explanation }

The smallest number of these books is ⑤ . ⑤ should be placed on the far left, so swap it with the ㉝ book. The position of ⑤ is confirmed.

**Find the smallest number**

Swap ㉝ and ⑤

**First swap**

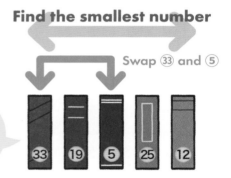

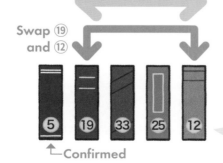

**Find the smallest number**

Swap ⑲ and ⑫

The next smallest number, ⑫, should be swapped with ⑲ in the position second from the left.

**Second Swap**

Confirmed

The next smallest number is ⑲. This book will be swapped with ㉝ which is the position third from the left.

**Find the smallest number**

Swap ㉝ and ⑲

**Third swap**

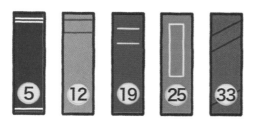

⑤ ⑫ ㉝ ㉕ ⑲

Confirmed

⑤ ⑫ ⑲ ㉕ ㉝

The next smallest number, ㉕ is already in the correct position. Finally, ㉝ is already positioned on the far right, so all the swaps are done. Only three swaps were required to line the books up in order.

Even though this and the cats were both sorting, the method was different!

# Let's Rearrange Books ②

## [Selection sort]

 Phew, I was wondering what to do because of my bad back, so I'm grateful that you rearranged the books so quickly.

 No problem! Would you like us to line up all the books in your house?

 Are you sure? That's very kind of you.

 Please have a seat and rest, sir.

 Wow, you two have really grown a lot!

**Question 16**

Rearrange the randomly ordered books so they are in ascending order. If you follow the rules, what is the lowest number of swaps needed to line up the books in numerical order?

# Swap books and line them up in ascending order from left to right

## {Rules}

● Find the book with the smallest number and swap it with the book on the far left. Among the remaining books, find the book with the smallest number and again swap it with the book on the far left.

● Repeat until all the books are lined up in order.

First, look for the book with the smallest number!

You really helped me! Thank you very much!

## ───────{ **Explanation** }───────

The smallest number within these books is ② . ② should be placed on the far left, so swap it with the ⑧ book. The position of ② is confirmed.

**Find the smallest number**

Swap ⑧ and ②

**First swap**

⑧ ㉒ ② ㊵ ㉜ ⑬

··················································································

**Find the smallest number**

Swap ㉒ and ⑧

The next smallest number, ⑧, should be swapped with ㉒ in the position second from the left.

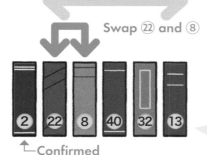

**Second Swap**

② ㉒ ⑧ ㊵ ㉜ ⑬

↑—Confirmed

**Find the smallest number**

Swap ㉒ and ⑬

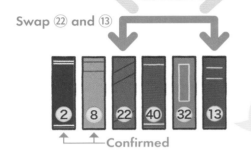

Confirmed

**Third swap**

The next smallest number is ⑬. This book will be swapped with ㉒ which is the position third from the left.

The next smallest number is ㉒. This book will be swapped with ㊵ which is the position third from the right.

**Find the smallest number**

Swap ㊵ and ㉒

**Fourth swap**

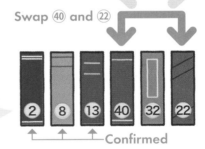

Confirmed

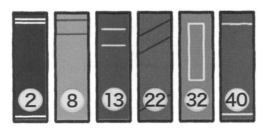

The next smallest number, ㉜ is already in the correct position. ㊵ is also positioned correctly, so four swaps were required to line the books up in order.

# Let's Find a Shortcut to the Park

## [Dijkstra's algorithm]

**Hero**

Oh nooooo! I'm late! I'm late!

That guy is wearing a unique costume.

Do you know a shortcut to the park? I have a "Hero Show" in the park now, but I think I'm going to be late! I need to stop by the warehouse, pick up some stuff and head to the park...

Somehow you don't seem like a hero. I'll find a shortcut to the park, so first calm down!

**Question 17**

Find the quickest route from the start to the park via the warehouse. The numbers on the map show the minutes it takes to walk each path. How long does it take to get to the park using the quickest route?

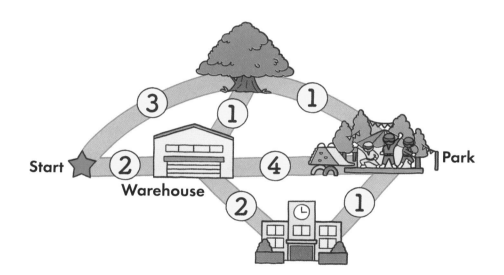

Start

Warehouse

Park

## {Rules}

● Find the quickest route for both "start to warehouse" and "warehouse to park."
● You cannot use the same path twice.

Wow! I think I'll arrive just in time! You really helped me out!

## { Explanation }

In order to find the quickest route from the start to the park via the warehouse, you need to find both "the quickest route from start to warehouse" and "the quickest route from warehouse to park".

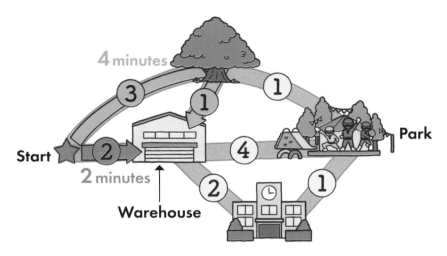

There are two routes from the start to the warehouse, a route which takes 4 minutes and a route which takes 2 minutes, so the 2 minute route is the quickest one.

Next, think about the route from the warehouse to the park. There are three routes, a route which takes 2 minutes, a route which takes 4 minutes, and a route which takes 3 minutes, so the 2 minute route is the quickest.

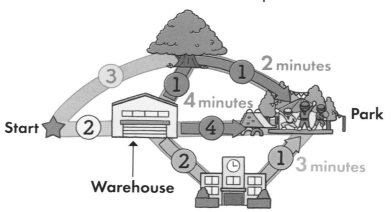

The shortest route from the start to the warehouse is 2 minutes, and the shortest route from the warehouse to the park is 2 minutes, so the total is 4 minutes. We found that the quickest possible route to get from the start to the park via the warehouse is 4 minutes.

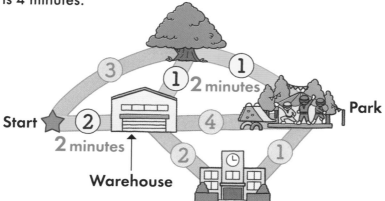

# Let's Find a Shortcut to the Park 2
## (Dijkstra's algorithm)

 Oh no! I forgot something!

 You're forgetful like me.

 I'm sorry to say this after you showed me that shortcut to the park, but I want to stop by a convenience store, too.

 There should be a lot of convenience stores around here! Let's find a shortcut to the park one more time!

**Question 18**

**Find the quickest route from the start to the park via the warehouse and the convenience store. The numbers on the map show the minutes it takes to walk each path. How long does it take to get to the park using the quickest route?**

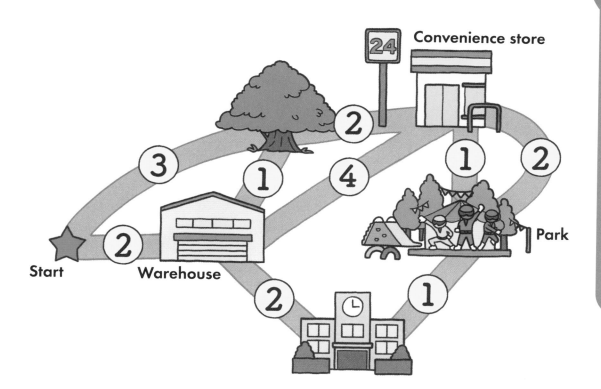

Convenience store

Park

Start

Warehouse

---

## {Rules}

- Find the quickest route for each of "start to warehouse," "warehouse to convenience store," and "convenience store to park."
- You cannot use the same path twice.

Answer ▶ **6 minutes**

 I would have been at a loss if I'd been alone. You saved me!

 Good luck at the Hero show!

---

## { Explanation }

---

First, find the quickest "start to warehouse" route.

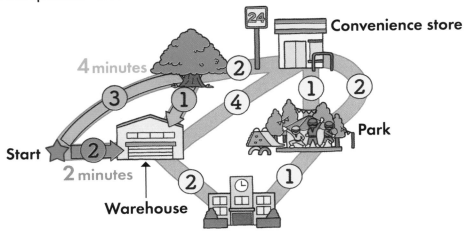

There are two routes from the start to the warehouse, a route which takes 4 minutes and a route which takes 2 minutes, so the 2 minute route is the quickest one.

---

Next, choose the "warehouse to convenience store" route. There are three routes, a route which takes 3 minutes, a route which takes 4 minutes, and a route which takes 5 minutes, so the 3 minute route is the quickest.

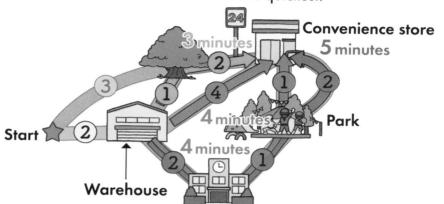

There are 3 "convenience store to park" routes, a route which takes 1 minute, a route which takes 2 minutes and a route which takes 7 minutes, so the 1 minute route is the quickest. We found out that the quickest possible route to get from the start to the park is 6 minutes (the total of 2 minutes, 3 minutes, and 1 minute).

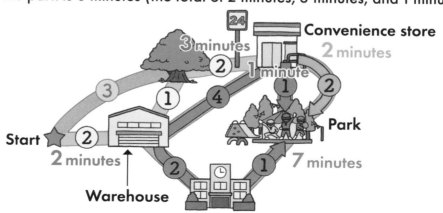

# Let's Send Secret Messages
## [Caesar cipher]

Lucas

Uhhh... I need help with something.

Oh, that's Lucas from the next class. What happened?

We are going to give a birthday present to our homeroom teacher next week. I want to tell my classmates about the present without the teacher finding out... Is there a good way to do it?

I've got a good idea! How about encrypting the message?

**Question 19**

Read a message from friends. The important word was encrypted (red letters) in case somebody might see it. Use the key set in [3] to decipher the message. Which one is the original message? Choose from options (1) to (3).

BEEP BEEP
ENCRYPTED

**Key : [3]**

**Send** ●●●●
~~~~~~~~~~~~~~~~
**Send** FDNH

(1) ball          (2) cake          (3) pens

---

# {Rules}

- Each letter is encrypted by moving later in the alphabet by the number of places shown in the key.

 ★ **If the key is [3]**

HOME → JQOG

Original word          Encrypted word

From "H" move two letters later in the alphabet → "J"
From "O" move two letters later in the alphabet → "Q"
From "M" move two letters later in the alphabet → "O"
From "E" move two letters later in the alphabet → "G"
Encrypted as "JQOG"

 **(2) cake**

 Wow! This will never be found out!

---

### { Explanation }

---

Decipher the encrypted word "FDNH" by using the key. The key is [3], so move the encrypted letters 3 letters earlier in the alphabet to find the original word.

Encrypted word

**S e n d** F D N H

↓

**Move F, D, N, and H
3 letters earlier in the alphabet**

If you're having trouble,
use the alphabet table.

**alphabet table**

| A | B | C | D | E | F | G | H | I | J | K | L | M | N | O | P | Q | R | S | T | U | V | W | X | Y | Z |

**Move three letters earlier**

 C D E  F  G

The letters were moved later in the alphabet when they were encrypted, so now move them earlier in the alphabet. F becomes C.

---

If D moves 3 letters earlier, it becomes A.

**Move three letters earlier**

 A B C D  E

---

**Move three letters earlier**

 K L M  N O

 E F G   H I

We find that N becomes K and H becomes E. When we connect all the letters, they spell CAKE, so the answer is (2) CAKE.

# Let's Send Secret Messages ②
## [Caesar cipher]

 Encrypting sounds cool! So exciting.

 If you use this, you can even send longer messages without being found out.

 Great! I'll send a secret message to my classmates about the surprise present for the teacher.

**Question 20**

**Set the key to [3] and send a secret message to friends. This is to tell them the details of the surprise present for the teacher, so the important words were encrypted (red letters) to prevent the secret being found out. What are the encrypted words?**

Details of the surprise present

## A drawing of WHDFKHU'V IDFH

ENCRYPTING
COMPLETE!

## Key : [3]

**Send** ●●●●●●●'● ●●●●

A drawing of **WHDFKHU'V IDFH**

---

## {Rules}

Each letter is encrypted by moving later in the alphabet by the number of places shown in the key.

 **★ If the key is [1]**

After Z it loops around again to A!

## BUZZ ⟶ CVAA

Original word        Encrypted word

From B move 1 letter later in the alphabet    → **C**

From U move 1 letter later in the alphabet    → **V**

From Z move 1 letter later in the alphabet    → **A**

From Z move 1 letter later in the alphabet    → **A**

Encrypted as **CVAA**

---

## Answer — A drawing of **teacher's face**

 Now all the preparations are complete! I feel like I can surprise the teacher!
Thank you very much for teaching me this useful skill.

 You're welcome. I hope your gifts make your teacher happy!

--- { **Explanation** } ---

Decipher the encrypted words using the key. The key is [3], so move the encrypted letters 3 places earlier in the alphabet to find the original word.

### A drawing of **WHDFKHU'V IDFH**

**Move 3 letters earlier**

**Move 3 letters earlier**

The letters were moved later in the alphabet when they were encrypted, so now move them earlier in the alphabet. The key is 【3】, so move all letters three places earlier in the alphabet, "WHDFKHU'V" becomes "TEACHER'S."

Move IDFH three places earlier in the alphabet, which becomes "FACE."

Now we know the message is "A drawing of teacher's face."

**Move 3 letters earlier**

# Algorithms and programming

The machines and home appliances around us cannot move according to their own will as humans do. The computers inside them are set to work according to the situation. Instructing computers to make these machines work as you wish is called programming.

Computers can complete a movement by following a set of instructions. Programming requires an aim and step-by-step instructions to make the computer understand.

✕ **State only aim**

I want you to bring me a pen

✓ **State aim and steps**

Open the door to the room
↓
Look at the items on the desk
↓
Find the blue pen
↓
Bring it to me

I'VE GOT IT!

It is useful to use flowcharts (p. 68) which make it easy to understand the flow of programming.

In Chapter 3 we learned algorithms which are used to sort a large amount information and line it up in order (p. 74 Bubble sort, p. 82 Selection sort), algorithms which are used to find the shortest route from start to finish (p. 90 Dijkstra's algorithm), and algorithms which are used to send secret messages so the content is not understood by others (p. 98 Caesar cipher).

Algorithms are not only used in machines or programming. For example, you rearrange things using sorting algorithms (Bubble sort or Selection sort), when you rearrange the cards in your hand to get them in numerical order when playing card games or rearrange documents in order of student number. I suspect that you also use search algorithms (Linear search or Binary search) when trying to find a word in a dictionary or looking for a book in the library. We use algorithms in our lives without even knowing it.

We have been using algorithms
this whole time!

## Algorithms in everyday items

It is possible to arrange songs in a music player by artist, song title, or popularity. It is easier to find specific songs when they are in order and it is also easier to get information, such as popularity. Sort algorithms are used here. There are many types of sort algorithms, so if the wrong one is used, it can take a long time to put the songs in order.

**Music player**

**Navigation by map app or GPS**

Map apps and GPS search for and show you the best route to your destination. Even when there may be a more direct route, using a route which looks like a detour can sometimes shorten your travel time. It is also possible to have settings which avoid routes with hills when walking, or find the shortest route when traveling by train or bus. Dijkstra's algorithm, among others, is used for calculating the shortest route.

It's all thanks to algorithms that these things are so convenient.

# Chapter 4

# Let's Master Algorithms

**A complete review of the algorithms we have learned.
These questions are more difficult than the previous ones,
so let's go slowly while reviewing the basics.**

One week after they started helping others

Hmm...... The sun will set soon...

That's right, we helped a lot of people again today. Let's go home shortly.

AHHHH

Everyone, look! QUICK's light bulb!

SHINE!

The light is on!!

# Let's Decide the Route Home
## (Sequential)

 Okaaay! We need to think about the route back to PLANET QUICK!

 You set off before figuring out our route?

 How should we get back to PLANET QUICK from Earth?

 It looks like there are several routes back to PLANET QUICK.

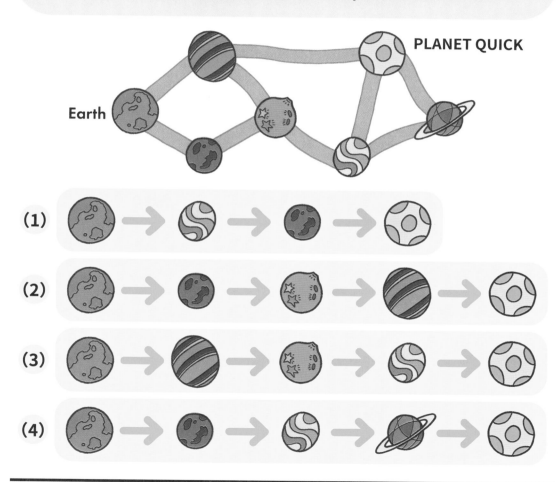

**Question 21**

Think about the route back to PLANET QUICK. Which routes out of options (1) to (4) can get you back to PLANET QUICK? Choose all possible answers from options (1) to (4).

 So we need to go via various planets to get to PLANET QUICK.

## { Explanation }

Check whether it is possible to get from Earth to PLANET QUICK by the routes shown.

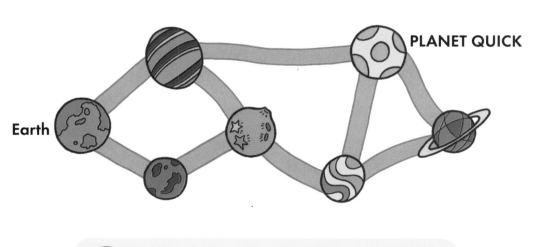

PLANET QUICK

Earth

(1)  ✗

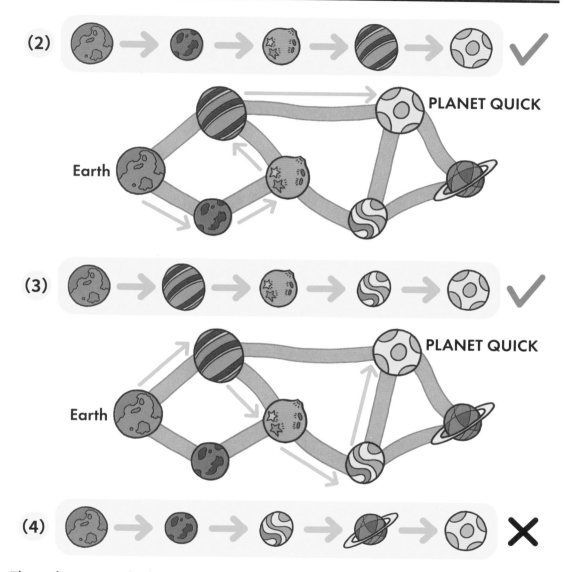

The only routes which reach PLANET QUICK are (2) and (3).

# Let's Decide the Route Home ②

## [Dijkstra's algorithm]

 Oh! There was something my mom asked me to do.

 What was it?

 I need to run some errands at PLANET BEEP.

 Hmm, then we need to find the quickest route to PLANET QUICK via PLANET BEEP.

 Can we get home quickly?

**Question**
**22**
Look for the quickest route to PLANET QUICK. How long does it take to get from Earth to PLANET QUICK via PLANET BEEP if we take the quickest route?

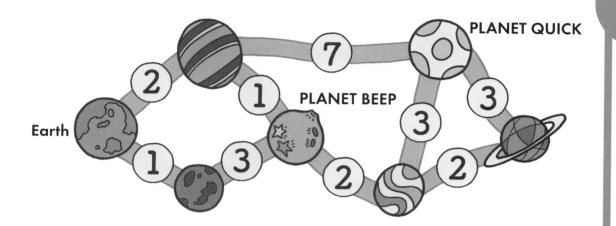

PLANET QUICK

PLANET BEEP

Earth

We need to go via PLANET BEEP to run errands!

## {Rules}

- The numbers show how many hours it takes to travel each path.
- Choose the quickest route for both "Earth to PLANET BEEP" and "PLANET BEEP to PLANET QUICK."
- You cannot use the same path twice.

**Answer** **8 hours**

 Okaaay, once again, we're ready to leave for PLANET BEEP!

---
{ **Explanation** }
---

Find the quickest route for both "Earth to PLANET BEEP" and "PLANET BEEP to PLANET QUICK."

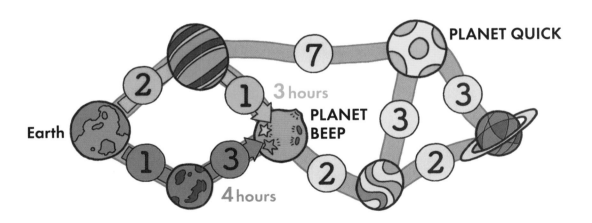

There are two routes from Earth to PLANET BEEP, a route which takes 4 hours and a route which takes 3 hours, so choose the 3 hour route.

Next, choose the quickest route from PLANET BEEP to PLANET QUICK. There are two routes, a route which takes 5 hours and a route which takes 7 hours, so the 5 hour route is quicker.

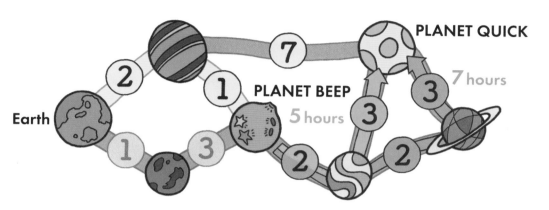

The quickest route from Earth to PLANET BEEP takes 3 hours, the quickest route from PLANET BEEP to PLANET QUICK takes 5 hours, so now we know the quickest route from Earth to PLANET QUICK takes 8 hours.

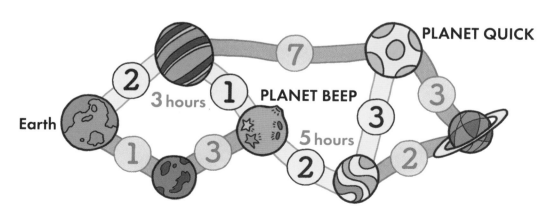

# Let's Run Errands ①
## (Caesar cipher)

 Pheeew. Finally, we arrived at PLANET BEEP.

 Wow, so this is PLANET BEEP. The atmosphere sure is different from Earth. By the way, what is your errand?

 I have a note from Mom. What?
The words are encrypted! My mom's favorite number is 4, so... the key should be 4!

**Question 23**

Decipher the encrypted words (red letters) using the key [4]. What are the original words encrypted in ① and ②?

Find a ① **WQEPP** ② **QYWLVSSQ**
on PLANET BEEP and bring
it with you.

From Mom

Key : [4]

ERRAND
DETAILS

## {Rules}

- Each letter is encrypted by moving forward in the alphabet by the number of places shown in the key.
- After Z it loops around again to A.

**Answer** ① **small** ② **mushroom**

 So my mom tested me to check whether my ability had improved or not. This question was too easy!

## { Explanation }

Decipher the encrypted words using the key. The letters were moved forward when they were encrypted, so move them back by the number of places shown in the key.

Find a ① **WQEPP** ② **QYWLVSSQ** on PLANET BEEP and bring it with you.

**Move back 4 letters.**

The key is **[4]**, so move each letter back 4 places and ①WQEPP becomes SMALL.

**Move back 4 letters**

··· **S** T U V **W** ···
··· **M** N O P **Q** ···
··· **A** B C E **D** ···
··· **L** M N O **P** ···
··· **L** M N O **P** ···

**Move back 4 letters**

··· **M** N O P **Q** ···
··· **U** V W X **Y** ···
··· **S** T U V **W** ···
··· **H** I J K **L** ···
··· **R** S T U **V** ···
··· **O** P Q R **S** ···
··· **O** P Q R **S** ···
··· **M** N O P **Q** ···

Next, change ②QYWLVSSQ back to the original word. Move all letters back 4 places to find MUSHROOM.

The message was SMALL MUSHROOM.

GREAT GREAT!

# Let's Run Errands ❶

## (Bubble sort, Selection sort)

 Oh, yeah! Mom said that mushrooms grown in PLANET BEEP are really valuable. Apparently, the smaller the tastier.

 I see, actually there are a lot of mushrooms growing. Should we pick some and line them up in size order?

 Errrrr, which method is the quickest to get them in order this time?

**Question 24** The mushrooms have stickers on them showing their height in centimeters. Line them up in ascending size order from left to right. The alien and the doctor will use different methods to sort the mushrooms. Which method will be quicker?

I'm going to use the Bubble sort method from p. 74. I'll compare the size of the mushroom on the far right with the mushroom next to it and, if the size of the mushroom on the left is bigger than the one on the right, I'll swap them. I'll repeat this until all the mushrooms are lined up in order.

**Doctor's method**

**Compare from the far right**

I'm going to use the Selection sort method from p. 82. I'll find the smallest mushroom and swap it with the mushroom on the far left.
Next, I'll find the smallest remaining mushroom...and repeat.

**Alien's method**

**Find the smallest number and swap**

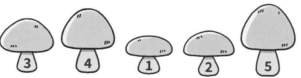

(1) Doctor　　(2) Alien　　(3) Same

## {Rules}

⬤ Each time you swap mushrooms, add one to your count. Choose the method which gets the mushrooms in order with the smallest count.

## Answer ▸ (2) Alien

Depending on the situation, it's best to change which algorithm you use. I may as well take the mushrooms back in a neat order.

---

{ **Explanation** }

---

Think about how many swaps it will take to line the mushrooms up in order using the doctor's method.

............................................................

**Doctor's method**

Compare the size of the mushrooms on the far right with the mushroom next to it and, if the mushroom on the left is bigger than the right one, swap their positions.

If you compare the two mushrooms on the far right, the 5 cm one on the right is bigger, so there is no need to swap. There is no need to swap the next 1 cm and 2 cm mushrooms either.

**Compare from the far right**

3   4   1   2   5

---

## First Swap

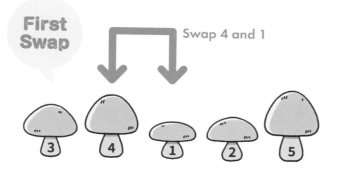

Swap 4 and 1

Next, the 4 cm mushroom on the left is bigger than the 1 cm mushroom on the right, so swap their positions.

Next, compare mushrooms on the far left. The 3 cm mushroom on the left is bigger than the 1 cm mushroom on the right, so swap them. We've compared all the mushrooms up to the far left, so the smallest mushroom is confirmed.

## Second swap

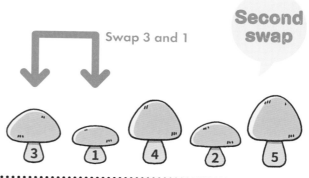

Swap 3 and 1

**Compare from the far right**

## Third Swap

Swap 4 and 2

Confirmed

Compare from the far right again. There is no need to swap 2 cm and 5 cm. Comparing the 4 cm and the 2 cm mushrooms, the 4 cm mushroom on the left is bigger, so swap their positions.

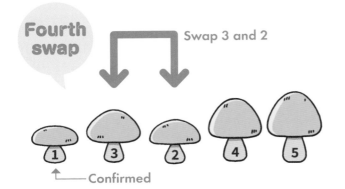

**Fourth swap**

Swap 3 and 2

Confirmed

Finally, comparing the 3 cm and 2 cm mushrooms, the 3 cm mushroom on the left is bigger, so swap their positions. The far left end has been confirmed, so all the swaps are done.

Next, let's line up the mushrooms using the alien's method.

**Alien's method**

Find the smallest mushroom and swap it with the mushroom on the far left. Next, find the smallest remaining mushroom...and repeat.

The smallest mushroom is the 1 cm one, swap it with the mushroom on the far left.

**Find the smallest number**

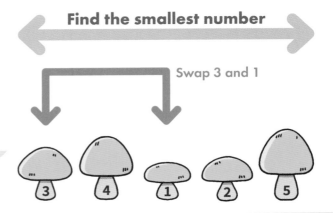

Swap 3 and 1

**First Swap**

**Find the smallest number**

Swap 4 and 2

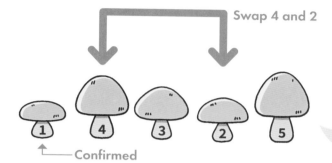

↑——Confirmed

The mushroom on the far left has been confirmed as the smallest one. The next smallest mushroom is the 2 cm one. Swap it with the 4 cm mushroom in the position second from the left.

**Second swap**

With this, the alien has lined up all the mushrooms in size order. The alien needed only two swaps and the doctor needed 4 swaps to line them up, so (2) the alien could line them up quicker.

Using selection sort was more efficient in this situation!

# Let's Help the Troubled Alien

## [Facility location problems]

**Girl from PLANET BEEP**

Ahhh! What should I do?

Oh, is that a girl from PLANET BEEP? She seems to be in trouble.

What happened?

Please help me! My flower beds were destroyed by animals!

Ummm...... oh yeah! How about using scarecrows to scare the animals away?

## Question 25

In order to prevent the flower beds being destroyed by animals, place scarecrows so they can directly see all of the flower beds. You can place scarecrows on the red circles (●) in the plan. What is the smallest number of scarecrows required?

## Plan of possible locations for scarecrows

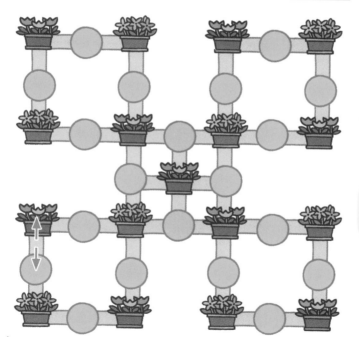

It is better to place scarecrows where they can see two flower beds.

There are many areas with a similar shape so there should be some regularity.

\* Adjoining flower beds can be seen by a scarecrow.

 You're from PLANET QUICK, right?
The rumor was true, you found the solution quick.

 Haha. You're welcome. Thanks to all of this practice, I may be closer to coming of age.

## { Explanation }

Let's divide the whole area into 5 sections to solve the question. There are lots of options in the center, so we will think about that later. First, place scarecrows in the top left section.

There are 2 options for the corner flower beds.

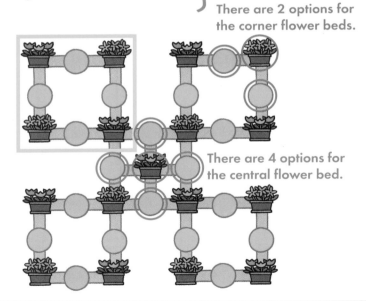

There are 4 options for the central flower bed.

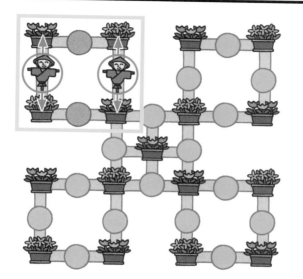

The key is placing a scarecrow where it can see two flower beds.

If scarecrows are placed in locations facing each other, each scarecrow can protect two flower beds.

Similarly, place two scarecrows facing each other in the top right section as well.

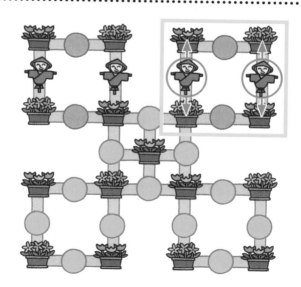

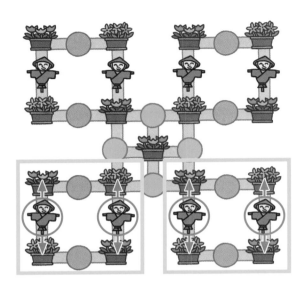

The bottom two sections have the same structure, so place two scarecrows in each area.

Finally, think about where to place scarecrows in the center. Except for the central section, all other flower beds are protected by scarecrows, so place one scarecrow on any of the red circles (⬤) to protect the central flower bed.

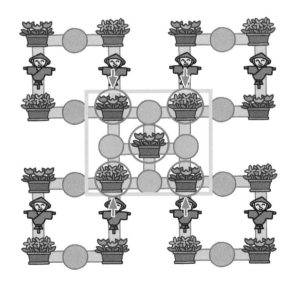

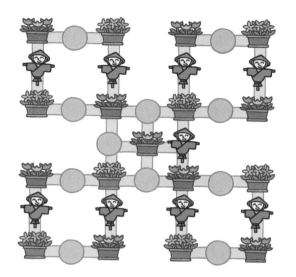

Now, all of the flower beds are protected by scarecrows.
We found that 9 scarecrows are required.

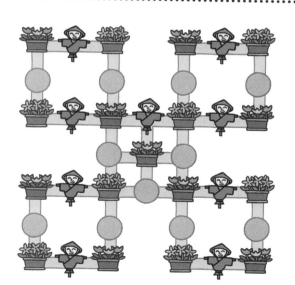

*The solution on the right is also correct.

**The End**

# From the Reviewer

**Algorithms are ways of thinking that help you make efficient programs and give you the ability to think logically.**

This book contained information about algorithms and programming, which are the basics of computing. As you know, computers can access the internet, everybody has a smartphone, and recently, artificial intelligence has greatly progressed such that it is improving our lives. As the years have progressed, computer technology has totally changed, but fundamental arithmetic has not changed. The way in which a computer thinks about this unchanging arithmetic is called an algorithm.

One of the advantages of computers is that they can accurately and efficiently perform complicated processes or process large amounts of data. This book explained Bubble sort (p. 74) and Selection sort (p. 82) as algorithms which rearrange data in ascending order. These algorithms which change the order of data are called Sorting algorithms. Thanks to sorting algorithms, we can read a larger number of emails or messages in order of date or sender.

I hope that while enjoying learning with this book, you will naturally learn about algorithms and programming. If you master the algorithmic way of thinking, you will be able to think logically and, as a result, you will be able to devise efficient steps or processes for work. I hope you will learn the skills to become adept at using computers.

**Professor of Osaka Electro-Communication University,**
**Vice President**
**Susumu Kanemune**

# List of Algorithms

Let's review algorithms.
There are many other types of algorithms which were not introduced in this book.

## What is the basic structure of an algorithm?

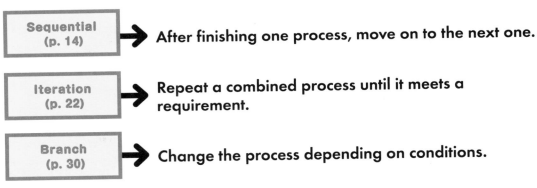

| Sequential (p. 14) | → After finishing one process, move on to the next one. |

| Iteration (p. 22) | → Repeat a combined process until it meets a requirement. |

| Branch (p. 30) | → Change the process depending on conditions. |

## Search algorithms

Search for target data from a range of data

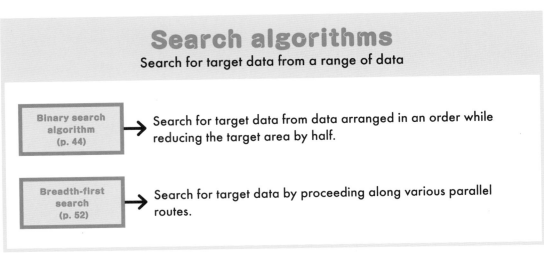

| Binary search algorithm (p. 44) | → Search for target data from data arranged in an order while reducing the target area by half. |

| Breadth-first search (p. 52) | → Search for target data by proceeding along various parallel routes. |